In memory of my Papa,
who would have turned eighty in 2007,
like Joseph Ratzinger.

To my Mama, with affection and gratitude.

Thanks to Father Georg Gänswein for the affectionate words that he wanted to offer to the readers of this book.

Story by
JEANNE PEREGO

Illustrations by
DONATA DAL MOLIN CASAGRANDE

Translated by
ANDREW MATT

Joseph and Chico

The Life of Pope Benedict XVI as Told by a Cat

Introduction by
FATHER GEORG GÄNSWEIN

IGNATIUS PRESS   SAN FRANCISCO

Original Italian edition © Copyright 2007 by P.P.F.M.C.
Messaggero di Sant'Antonio-Editrice
Basilica del Santo, Via Orto Botanico, 11
35123 Padua, Italy

Page layout by Roberto Chillon and Beljan, Ltd.
Cover design by Giuliano Dinon

© 2008 Ignatius Press, San Francisco
All rights reserved
ISBN 978-1-58617-252-7
Printed in Canada ∞

Introduction

by FATHER GEORG GÄNSWEIN

(Private secretary of the Pope)

Joseph and Chico: *this is the title of the book you are about to read. It is a book with many pictures about the life of a most unique person: the Holy Father.*

So many things are written and said about the Pope each day! But here, dear children, you have a biography unlike any other because it is told by a cat, and it's not every day that you find a cat who can call himself a friend of the Holy Father and who decides to write his life's story.

They have each known one another for quite some time and it is extremely interesting to hear what sorts of things Chico has to say, always from his own point of view, obviously. After all, he is a cat, even if he is a cat friend.

It has been several years now since I started working alongside Pope Benedict XVI, and my name is Father Georg—Father George in English—just like the Holy Father's older brother. I can assure you that everything you will find in this book written for you by Jeanne Perego, illustrated by Donata Dal Molin Casagrande, and published by Ignatius Press is all true and interesting. So let us thank these friends who have gathered this story and these pictures together into a beautiful and easy-to-read book for you.

Reading these pages I became excited by how many other things I could and would like to add! To begin with, I agree with the fact that the Holy Father is a special person, but it is above all because he is a real friend of Jesus. This is important! Here is the secret of his life: only by becoming a true friend of Jesus can we learn to open our hearts to the people we meet and to all the people of the world. Isn't it true, as you see on television, that Pope Benedict never stops repeating that love is the secret to joy and peace in the world, that only Love, that is, God, can fulfill the desires of our hearts and give meaning to our human lives?

Precisely because he is filled with trust in Jesus, the Pope is not discouraged by difficulties and never gets tired of loving everyone. In a special way, children, he loves you all, and he also knows that, with a little effort, you know how to be generous. Better yet, he prays every day that you may grow up to be healthy and good in body and soul. You will then be happy and be able to make the world a better place.

Of course, the Pope also loves cats and all animals because they are God's creatures, and often, like Chico, they can teach us things that are worth hearing. For example, as our friend Chico ends his story, he tells us that he understands now that the Holy Father is no longer just his personal friend, but the great friend and guide to all Catholics. Chico, who is a cat, even understands what the Pope's real mission is: to be the friend of all people in the way that Jesus was, who loved so much that he gave his life on the Cross for us. This is not only the Pope's mission but that of all Christians, of all those, that is, who choose Jesus as their best friend. This is a mission for big people, but also for little ones like you, because love knows no age limits. God is Love.

Vatican City, July 4, 2007   FATHER GEORG GÄNSWEIN

Joseph and Chico

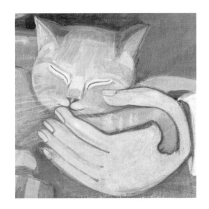

MEEEOOOOW! I'm Chico, and who are you?

I am a tabby cat, one of the most common cats on the prowl. I'm sure this is not the first time you've come across a tabby. But I doubt you've ever known one quite like me: really cute, with a big beautiful coat of ginger fur. Okay, so I'm a little vain. But all cats are a bit vain—you knew that, didn't you?

I'm meeting you in the pages of this book to tell you a story about my very best friend, a wonderful man with whom I've shared so many happy times. He is such an extraordinary person that his story shouldn't be kept only between the two of us. I want to tell you about where he comes from, how devoted he is to his studies and work, what he is doing now. . . . In short, I want him to become your friend too, as well as mine.

Unfortunately, he now lives far away from me, because that's how human life goes sometimes. Every now and then they have to do things that take them far away, even from their favorite cats. Stuff that's hard to believe. . . .

Lately I've heard that my friend now has such important commitments that it will be difficult for him to return and visit me like he did in the past. Meeeooow! This is really bad news! It's as if someone had told me that all mice, spiders, and kitty treats had disappeared from the face of the earth.

Even though he cannot come to visit me any more, I'm sure he still loves me a whole lot. In fact, do you know what? I've been told that he often asks about me. But the way he used to pet me and the sweet Bavarian phrases he used to whisper in my ear. . . . These are the things I really, really miss. By the way, Bavarian is the dialect the humans speak where I live. We Bavarian cats communicate in cat talk like every other feline around the world; our accent is just a little rougher, that's all.

The story about my friend begins on April 16, 1927, on an extremely chilly night. Brrrrrrr, don't make me think about it, for we cats can't stand the cold. As soon as I feel a shiver run across my fur coat, I race for the kitchen, which is the warmest room in the house where I've chosen to live. Because, let's be clear about this: cats choose the owners they live with, not the other way around, as humans tend to imagine.

At 4:15 that morning, in house number eleven on the town square of Marktl-on-Inn, here in Bavaria, the strong cry of a newborn baby was heard. Joseph Aloysius had come into the world, the third child of Maria and Josef. The might of his screams made one

thing immediately clear: this boy would know how to make himself heard. Further-more, he had arrived on a special day, none other than the eve of Easter.

Early the following morning, Mama Maria and Papa Josef got ready to take their new baby to the church to be baptized. Maria and Georg, the older sister and brother, who were six and two years old, ran all over the place hunting for their coats. "I'm sorry, children, but you won't be able to come", Mama told them. "It's much too cold outside and you could catch cold." Not at all happy with this news, the two children went and pressed their noses against the icy window as they watched their parents cross the town square, holding baby Joseph tightly in their arms.

My friend spent two very happy years in Marktl. Of course, like all children, every so often he was a little naughty. Like that time just before Christmas, when he realized that the teddy bear in the storefront window that he had been admiring for days suddenly disappeared. "Where is my teddy bear? I want my teddy bear!" screamed Joseph as he kicked his feet against the empty window. He was in despair; he had been dreaming about that teddy bear almost every night. He simply loved furry animals. He had a dog, a duck, and a cat, but that teddy bear was the animal he wanted most. A surprise, however, was just around the corner. On December 25, when Maria, Georg, and Joseph gathered in the living room with their parents to celebrate Christmas, who should be sitting comfortably on the couch but . . . the teddy bear of Joseph's dreams!

Their tranquil life, unfortunately, did not last long. The first of a series of relocations were about to begin. Changing and moving from house to house have been the order of the day in my friend's life. I simply don't know how he's been able to tolerate such things. For us cats, who are terribly set in our ways and fond of certain smells, the idea of constantly having to move our milk bowl from here to there is utterly unacceptable. You've never seen a cat with a suitcase, right? Or a moving company for cats? Of course not. Just thinking about it gives my tail the cramps . . . .

You need to know that Joseph's father was a policeman. In short, his work involved making sure people respected all the laws. One day he announced to his wife, "Maria, we have to leave Marktl. I've been given a new job fifty miles away. But you don't have to worry; we'll have a nice big house there where we can raise our children." And so it was. Joseph's family packed up and moved to the town of Tittmoning.

Even today my friend still has a soft spot in his heart for that place. He's talked about it often with me. For example, he told me that at Christmas he and his brother would always build a beautiful nativity scene, using moss and twigs gathered in the woods and stones collected along the river. The brothers were not exactly what you would call engineering geniuses, but they knew how to construct convincing mountains and hills.

At the age of three, Joseph began to go to nursery school. One day, while he was at school, something extraordinary happened. A luxurious black car pulled up in front of the door. At the time, Joseph did not know that a car like that was called a limousine. Out of the car stepped a tall man, elegantly dressed. My friend had never seen anyone dressed like that before: he wore a long cassock made of beautiful red silk. And on his finger he had a marvelous golden ring that sparkled in the sunlight. The teachers told the children that he was a cardinal who had just arrived for the Confirmation class. Joseph observed him for a long time. Then, all of sudden, he exclaimed, "When I grow up I want to be a cardinal too!" But he soon forgot about this, since for a long while he also thought he wanted to be a house painter.

At Tittmoning Joseph also began to visit his church regularly, which was located behind the nursery school. Accompanied by his parents he discovered Advent, Christmas, Easter . . . . These special moments of the year would accompany him all his life.

He was almost six years old when he had to move again. At first Joseph and his siblings did not like Anschau-on-Inn very much, and it took a little time before all three of them began to grow fond of the beautiful new house with a garden. And it was precisely the garden that Joseph liked the most. There were lots of trees, many brightly colored flowers, and a pond filled with darting carp that almost became the scene of a tragedy. During that period my friend was very exuberant and did not miss a chance to get a little rambunctious. Like all children of his age he loved to run, jump, explore, roll on the ground. One day, while playing tag with his brother and sister—SPLASH!—he fell right into the fish pond. If they hadn't pulled him out in time he would have drowned. But it taught him a good lesson: from then on he paid close attention to where he put his feet.

In the town of Anschau, Joseph made his First Communion and learned how to play the piano. The sound of this musical instrument pleased him right away, and it became his great passion. Even now, as a grown-up, when he wants to relax he will sit down in front of the piano and play some Mozart, who seems to be his favorite composer. I can't really say a whole lot about this Mozart, but I do know that his music makes even a super-cat like me have better dreams. Whenever Joseph would pass through on a visit and play the piano, I would love to have some fun and walk along the keyboard a bit. Then, when I'd see him start to lose patience with me, I would curl up next to him and begin to purr, moving my tail in time to the music.

You won't believe it, but . . . then he had to move again! And this made three times. When my friend was ten years old, he and his family moved to a little town on the outskirts of Traunstein where Papa Josef had bought a house for them to live in when he retired. When Joseph saw it for the first time he thought, "Where have we ended up now?" In fact, the house had been neglected for a long time, so that it needed both a great deal of renovation and all the good will Mama Maria could muster in order for it to become a little corner of paradise. There was a big garden with many fruit trees and a lot of space to play and have fun. Inside the house, however, they lacked many conveniences that seem normal today, for example, running water. As a result, Joseph and the others had to go wash themselves in the drinking fountain outside the front door. Luckily we cats wash ourselves without water or soap, for I never would have been able to put up with all that going out and in again just to be clean.

One of the things my friend really loved to do was to study. He found such joy in sitting in front of a book, eyes glued to the pages, as he soaked up all the ideas and knowledge that he could. Thus, with great enthusiasm, he started high school that year in Traunstein. To get to school each day he had to walk nearly two miles on foot. And that's not easy, even in good weather! You can imagine how many times he found himself trudging along under rain or snow. . . .

At school he began to study Latin, an ancient language that cats do not learn because we don't have much use for it. For Joseph, however, it has proved very useful throughout his whole life. In fact, he even seems to speak Latin fluently. If you want to know how Latin sounds, then you should know that *mus* means mouse, *feles* means cat, and *sinus* means cat food bowl. Just between us, these are the most important words in every language, so it's best to learn them well.

In 1939 Joseph entered the seminary where his brother, Georg, was already living. This was a very important decision, the first step toward a life dedicated to Jesus. It was not easy for his family to undertake such a decision; it would have been impossible to pay the tuition for both sons with Papa Josef's modest ex-policeman's pension. Fortunately, during that time Maria, my friend's older sister, found a good job and with her income they were able to cover the expenses.

At the beginning, Joseph was not enthusiastic at all about living in a community. He could not concentrate on his studies and it felt as if he had lost his freedom. Not to mention gym class: every day he had to face two unbearable hours of stretches, sit-ups, push-ups, running, jumping. What a nightmare! I totally sympathize with him because we cats also detest strenuous physical activity. However, we always have to be in good shape; a mouse, a grasshopper, or a butterfly could appear suddenly and we need to be ready to pounce on our prey!

While Joseph and Georg set off toward what would become their future life in the Church, a tragedy was developing in Germany that would throw the whole world into turmoil. I'm talking about Nazism, one of the most dramatic and shameful moments in human history. Animals do not behave with the same ferocity as certain people did during that time. And you're listening to an animal talking who knows how to be fierce when necessary.

During that period Joseph was forced to do something that went absolutely against his will: join the army and go off to war.

We cats do not make war. We don't even know what wars are. In order to make other cats aware that they are crossing over into our territory, or that they are courting a cat who's already engaged to be married, we put on a threatening look, raise the fur on our backs,

pull out our tails, and screech at the top of our lungs, "RRRREEEOOOOOWWW!", which would frighten anyone. It's a shame that you humans are not so advanced.

At first Joseph was sent to guard an airplane motor factory and later to erect barriers against possible tank attacks. During that time he discovered what it meant to be afraid.

When the war ended, he found himself in a prison camp together with 50,000 other prisoners, forced to live in the open air on one piece of bread and a bowl of soup a day. Fortunately, after a few weeks they were liberated, and Joseph could finally go home. Life began to smile on him again, even though he still had to travel a hundred miles by foot before he could reach his destination.

While he was walking together with a companion who was going in the same direction, a pickup truck carrying milk cans passed them on the road and then pulled over. "Where are you fellows going?" asked the driver. "To Traunstein", the two responded. "You're in luck," the driver said. "That's just where I'm headed. Hop in the back, and I'll take you there myself." Thus it was that Joseph and his friend were able to see their loved ones before nightfall.

At the end of that year Joseph took up his studies again, now as a guest at the seminary of Freising, which stood right in front of a big beautiful church that still holds a special place in his heart. He liked these accommodations very much, especially the large library that miraculously was left unscathed by the war. For Joseph this proved to be an unforgettable time; he was able to read, read, and then read some more. If the expression didn't give me a stomachache, I'd have to say that my friend had become something of a "bookworm".

Besides Latin, Joseph studied theology and philosophy, two topics that are a bit too complicated for cats, but that helped my friend to deepen his love and knowledge of God and of how humans think. In less than no time, Joseph was ready to go college in Munich. And once again he found himself in a rather uncomfortable situation. In fact, the terrible bombardments during the war had almost completely destroyed the university buildings where he was supposed to take classes. So Joseph and his fellow classmates were sent to a small castle outside the city, which had been transformed temporarily into a college. Very little space was available, and his classes were held in an old greenhouse, which was freezing in the winter, Brrrrr! and boiling in the summer, Whew! Joseph, however, was so happy with his studies that he barely noticed all these discomforts.

The castle was surrounded by a large park, where my friend often took long walks when he was not studying. As he strolled through the woods and green fields, breathing in the rich smells of the earth and enjoying the play of sunlight that streamed through the tree branches, he thought about the things he had learned in class that day and about the important decisions he was getting ready to make in his life, such as his desire to become a priest and a teacher.

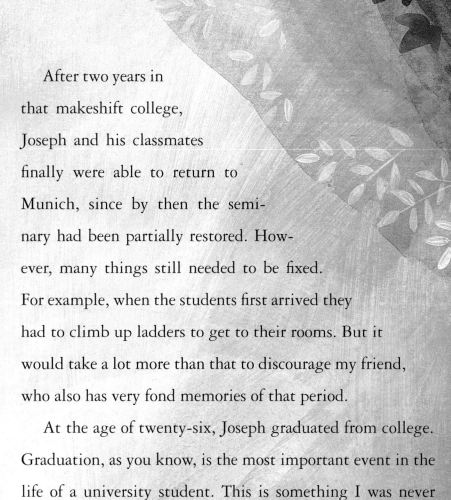

After two years in
that makeshift college,
Joseph and his classmates
finally were able to return to
Munich, since by then the seminary had been partially restored. However, many things still needed to be fixed.
For example, when the students first arrived they
had to climb up ladders to get to their rooms. But it
would take a lot more than that to discourage my friend,
who also has very fond memories of that period.

At the age of twenty-six, Joseph graduated from college.
Graduation, as you know, is the most important event in the
life of a university student. This is something I was never
able to experience because, unfortunately, there are no feline
universities. But if someone were to invent a cat college,
I'm absolutely positive that nobody could deny me a degree
in field mouse hunting. In fact, they could go ahead and
make me a professor right away.

In the meantime, another extremely important moment in Joseph's life had taken place. On June 29, 1951, he was ordained a priest in the Freising cathedral, the beautiful church that stood in front of the seminary he had attended as a young student. Together with Joseph was his brother Georg. Cardinal Faulhaber was the bishop who placed his hands on their heads, which happens during the ceremonies when priests are officially consecrated. This was the very person whom Joseph, as a little boy, had so admired in front of his nursery school!

When my friend thinks back on that day, one thing in particular comes to mind that always moves him. It moved me too when he told me about it. At the moment when the cardinal placed his hands on his head, a little bird flew right over him and began chirping happily. Doesn't that seem like a special sign to you? It appears that my friend was destined to become an important figure. And not just for me.

At this point Joseph began a new life, now from the other side of the teacher's lectern. In fact, he started teaching at the very same school in Freising where he had been a student a few years earlier.

It was not easy to gain such a position, for he had to overcome many obstacles. However, the idea of buying a house to live in with his parents, who were very old by now, gave him the courage and strength to face all of the difficulties. Joseph's house in Freising therefore became the house for his the entire family, including Georg and his sister Maria.

It's at this moment that a bear comes on the scene. What does a bear have to do with anything? Well, just wait and see. During his student years in Freising, Joseph had made the acquaintance of a bear—a bear who had won a piece of his heart almost as big as the one I had won. As a matter of fact, I have to admit that he became so fond of this bear that he wanted to take him everywhere he went.

What you need to know is that, nearly thirteen hundred years ago, a bishop of Freising named Corbinian was making a pilgrimage to Rome when he was attacked by a bear that tore to pieces the poor mule he was riding. Corbinian scolded the bear severely and forced him to load onto his back all the baggage that the mule had been carrying. They reached Rome without any problems, and on the way back to Freising the bishop released the bear, who went back happily to his life in the wild.

Corbinian eventually became the patron saint of Freising, in whose memory the bear who had carried the bishop's belongings became the centerpiece on the city's coat of arms. Joseph never forgot about that bear symbol.

But now let's return to our story, with Joseph and his family living together in Freising, while he taught there as a professor. At this point I would like to be able to say that "they all lived happily ever after." But I can't do that, because other changes were about to take place.

My friend was a really good professor—so good, in fact, that he was quickly made a teacher of future professors. In the process, he was asked to teach, one after the other, in three different German universities.

During that period, however, a protest movement began to spread throughout all the European universities as never before. Since Joseph is a quiet type of person, he was very unhappy in that situation. Then an offer came his way to teach at the University of Regensburg, where the students were not as agitated as everywhere else. As a result of these changing circumstances, his brother, Georg, also moved there to become music director of the Regensburg cathedral.

It was during this time that Joseph began to have a house built just outside the city at Pentling, which is right next door to where I live. We both met each other when I came to live here. Do you know how I found out he was a cat lover? Because he put a statue of a cat out in his backyard. Not the cutest cat in the world, but it was still a cat. If it had been a dog statue, you can be sure that I never would have set a paw in that yard!

Joseph taught at the university by day and devoted himself to reading and playing the piano by night. His classes were always packed: everyone wanted to hear what that professor had to say, the one who had also become vice president of the university. One day, in the middle of one of his classes, a messenger from Rome arrived with a letter.

During his years as a professor, Joseph had written some books and also had traveled frequently to the Vatican as an adviser at a huge meeting of all the bishops in the world, where many important decisions for the Catholic Church were made. There were so many topics to cover that the meeting lasted four years!

Listening to him speak and reading his books, the Pope and his colleagues realized that Joseph was a really smart person. That's why the messenger from Rome had arrived that day with a letter—a letter informing my friend that he had been appointed archbishop of Munich and Friesing. But that wasn't all; a few months later he was named Cardinal, which means a special co-worker with the Pope.

Every bishop chooses a personal coat of arms. Joseph wanted to display on his coat of arms the head of the "Moor of Freising", symbol of the bishops of that city for a thousand years; the conch shell that recalls one of his favorite saints, Saint Augustine; and the image of the animal that holds a special place in his heart. Did you say "a cat"? Nope, I'm sorry to say, even if I agree with you; a big beautiful ginger tabby would have cut quite a figure on that coat of arms. Instead of a cat, the third image Joseph wanted was Saint Corbinian's bear: the bear who was forced to lug the saint's belongings on his back all the way to Rome. That animal really found the way into my friend's heart!

At this point the story might have ended.

It might have—if Joseph had only stayed in Bavaria and then retired to his little house in Pentling, with the ugly statue of a cat in his backyard and the most beautiful tabby in the world as his neighbor. But destiny had other things in store for him.

At that time, the Pope was looking for someone to put in charge of a very important office at the Vatican. Take a wild guess at whom he picked. Joseph, of course. In 1981, the

30

Pope appointed him prefect, that is, the head, of that office. And in that moment began the collaboration, but above all the friendship, between Joseph and Pope John Paul II.

A little sad because he had to leave the land in which he had been born and raised, but happy because of his new mission, Joseph moved, once again—this time to Rome.

Once there, he worked more than ever; he wrote books and articles, prepared official documents, held conferences and classes, organized meetings with important people, studied, listened, lectured, read, read, read. . . . When he got tired, really tired, he would head north and come back here for a rest. When I'd see that the shades were up next door, I knew he was home. Then I'd race over and rub up against his legs. What wonderful times we've spent together. . . .

Every once in a while I'd get a little frisky with him too. One Christmas I think I may have even scratched him. He wanted to send me outside to get a breath of fresh air, but I was not about to budge from the cozy spot I'd found on his couch, so I let him have a good look at my long nails. He quickly forgave me. "But don't do that again", he told me, and the only thing he mentioned to my caretakers is that I act a little crazy now and then.

On April 2, 2005, Pope John Paul II died. Joseph was filled with sorrow that day because he had lost a best friend as well as his longtime "boss". It turns out that Joseph was the one who celebrated the funeral Mass, for he had been the head of all the cardinals for some time. More than three million people listened to the funeral homily he gave in St. Peter's Square that day, while over ninety television stations transmitted his words live across the globe.

The Italians have a saying that goes like this: When one pope dies, you make another. In other words, life goes on. It's a little sad, but that's what happens; after the funeral of a pope, another one quickly needs to be elected because the Church cannot go on without someone to lead the way forward. In order to choose a new pontiff, all the cardinals meet together in the Sistine Chapel. None of them can leave the meeting until they are in agreement about which one among them should take on such an important task. Of course, they are allowed to eat, drink, sleep, and think about their cat (at least those fortunate enough to have one), but they can't go home until they have elected a new pope. First, the cardinals write down on a piece of paper the name of the one they want to be pope. Then they all wait to see if one of the candidates gets a majority vote. If so, the pieces of paper are burned in a stove together with some special powder that creates white smoke, which then goes out the chimney of a roof in St. Peter's Square. Otherwise, the powder they mix in turns the smoke black.

The little cloud of white smoke that announced to the world that a new Pope had been chosen appeared on April 19, 2005, in the late afternoon, which is when I normally get my cat food. My humans, along with everyone else, were glued to the television. "Say goodbye to your cat food tonight", I thought to myself. I was watching the TV too, and I was almost sure that the white smoke was curling into the shape of a smiling cat. Or maybe that was just the hunger pangs playing tricks with me.

After a little while, the window from which the name of the new pontiff is announced came open. Everyone was holding his breath as the one in charge of making these announcements read a very complicated sentence in Latin that, more or less, went like this: "Ladies and gentlemen, I am happy to inform you that we have a new Pope: Joseph Cardinal Ratzinger, who has chosen to be called Benedict XVI." A moment later, right out there on the balcony appeared my friend Joseph!

Our whole house was going crazy with joy, and we were all moved when we heard him greet everybody and thank the cardinals who had elected him to be the successor of Pope John Paul II. I was so excited that I actually forgot about asking for dinner that night.

We have now come to the end of the story I wanted to tell you. Do you understand why my friend Joseph no longer has any time to come visit me? Now Joseph Ratzinger is not only my friend, but also the great friend and leader of all Catholics. And what about me? I'm comforted by thinking about the journey Joseph has made from Marktl to Rome. He has shown how you need to stay faithful and committed in life, without getting discouraged when difficulties arise.

Now I have to leave you, because I'm in a hurry to check on my garden as well as my friend's. I want to make sure no mice have tried to sneak in while I've been telling you my story. I need to rush because those pesky rodents are always waiting for us cats to drop our guard in order to start some mischief!

MEEEOOOOWWW! Send my greetings to all the cats in your neighborhood and always remember to treat them as true friends: one of them might decide to tell a very special story one day—and it might be yours!